Let Not Your Hart

Let Not Your Hart

by JAMES SEAY

WESLEYAN UNIVERSITY PRESS

Middletown, Connecticut

PS
3569
E24 L4

Acknowledgement is gratefully made to the following periodicals, in the pages of which some of the poems in this volume were first published: *The Hollins Critic, Kansas Quarterly, The Mississippi Folklore Register, The New Orleans Review, Per/Se, The Roanoke Review, The Southern Review, The Virginia Quarterly Review,* and *The Western Humanities Review.*

Hardbound: SBN   8195   1050   5

Paperback: SBN   8195   2050   0

Library of Congress catalog card number: 71–105509

Manufactured in the United States of America

FIRST EDITION

For Lee

Contents

I. The Troubled Hart

Grabbling in Yokna Bottom : 11

In Your Footprint's Hourglass : 12

No Man's Good Bull : 13

Touring the Indian Dead : 14

Turtles from the Sea : 17

The Final Reasoning of Kings : 18

Water I Thought Sweet and Deep : 19

No Fluid-Fed Governor : 20

LET NOT YOUR HART BE TRUBLE : 22

II. Other Sides

Options : 27

The Majorette on the Self-Rising Flour Sign : 29

Through My Santa Mask : 31

The Barber with the California Tan : 33

The Feather : 34

The Lame, the Halt, the Half-Blind : 36

One Last Cheer for Punk Kincaid : 37

Departure from the Waldorf : 38

Valley of Dry Bones : 39

III. Light-Hearted

In My Secret Iago Heart

or

Renal Calculus : 43

The Adoration of the Magi : 44

My Dog and I Grow Fat : 45

No Doric Air : 46

I Circle the Midway : 47

Sweetbread and Wine : 49

Lines Composed a Few Miles below Princeton Junction : 50

IV. Turnings

Were You Wise, Awake? : 53

The Starlings : 54

The Room : 55

Else Birth Make Us Husband : 57

The Pomegranate : 59

Ring, Chain, Coin : 63

The Bells : 66

The Gars : 68

Toward Other Waters : 72

The Day Speedo Stole the Meat Wagon : 74

"Does Anybody Wanna Buy My Little Brother?" : 76

Languages We Are Not Born To : 79

The Big Money Comes to My Hometown : 80

The Bluebottle Tree : 81

Kelly Dug a Hole : 82

Circling the Reef : 84

Others of Rainbow Colors : 85

Moonwing : 86

DIAL DIRECT : 89

Turning toward Song : 91

1. The Troubled Hart

The hungry come in a dry time
To muddy the water of this swamp river
And take in nets what fish or eel
Break surface to suck at this world's air.

But colder blood backs into the water's wood —
Gills the silt rather than rise to light —
And who would eat a cleaner meat
Must grabble in the hollows of underwater stumps and roots,

Must cram his arm and hand beneath the scum
And go by touch where eye cannot reach,
Must seize and bring to light
What scale or slime is touched —

Must in that instant — on touch —
Without question or reckoning
Grab up what wraps itself cold-blooded
Around flesh or flails the water to froth,

Or else feel the fish slip by,
Or learn that the loggerhead's jaw is thunder-deaf,
Or that the cottonmouth's fangs burn like heated needles
Even under water.

The well-fed do not wade this low river.

In Your Footprint's Hourglass

I see you under mercury-vapor lights
Beside the road at night.
Your pale-as-vapor face, a small moon
Cratered with the acids of a long gone
Puberty, reflects no solar
Body as you watch familiar stars.

What you see in the dark
Beyond the mercury-vapor arc
I do not know — or what you seek
When from the sand ditch bank
You rise and go
To some familiar woman's window

Or from your mother's house
Beside the sand ditch mouth
You fix your telescope on distant bodies
I do not know — your eyes
Reflect no solvent lights.
No man will know the night

When lunar caustic filtered in
Your telescopic lens
Like sand and cauterized
The tissues of your eyes.
I can only see the tracks
On your sidewalk beside the ditch —

In your footprint's hourglass
The sand is standing still.

No man's good bull grazes wet clover
And leaves the pasture as he came.
My uncle's prize Angus was bloated
And breathing hard by afternoon
On the day he got into our clover pasture
Before the sun could burn the dew away.
He bellowed death from the field
As we grappled to hold his legs and head;
Our vet inserted a trocar between his ribs,
              let the whelming gas escape,
And to show us the nature of that gas
Put a match to the valve . . . a blue flame caught
       and the animal bolted from us,
Heading into the woods along the river bottom,
Turning only to test the new fire
              of his black side.

Each night we see his flame, blue and soft
              beside the river,
As he steals in before dawn
To plunge his head into wet clover,
Graze his fill,
      blaze up,
And answer that which lows to him in heat.
We watch him burn —
          hoof, hide, and bone.

Touring the Indian Dead

Sundered from the normal dead,
toward all drifts of the soul's compass
they point —
    the long-headed baby,
      an arthritic,
  two men, face down, head to toe and toe to head,
and then that most appalling attitude
    below this tourist ledge: the supine woman
        with a furrow half-mooning her skull —
none shriven, none graced as are their unearthed kin
in separate burials with magic trappings
    or memento discs where struck in stone
is a hand palming the all-seeing, sometimes weeping, eye —
souls waterless, without the pointed flint
    and vessels of their distant brother,
each laid to face whatever wild sun
        drove to this primeval shade,
    their postures, their directions
tracing in death the restless quiver of their flesh's needle.
     Drifting, drifting
  until the magnet of night
    draws me back,
I descend with its force into their marrow
    to wheel the thin ivory eastward
where to the coming sun can now be spoken
    their aboriginal grief —
all but one, all but one
    they speak,
their phosphorous words illumine the diorama
    of this village's dispossessed:

From the cretin jaw come words
of how sweet is even the wolf's breast
when a mother's dug is snatched away.
        In my ear is whispered terrible infant wisdom.

And age. I hear from the arthritic
how the eternal river boiled a vapor
that crooked and fused his spine,
        bent him into himself,
cast by the flood into a slew beneath the bitter willows.

The face-down pair break their tongue's dust:
        digging clams in the same river mud
    they found flesh to sate grave hunger,
denied an ever-thronging tribe their sodom progeny.
Buried beside them in a pile of mussel shells
I behold what is spawned in man's bowels by his own.
        It burrows into the wasting pearl.

They glow, they are speaking, all but one —
        young, carrying into dust
            the runnel mark
of a scalping healed over how many lunar winters,
her frail posture locked in this magnet's field,
she strains toward her own kindled fire,
        knowing the sufficient bead of its weld —
and yet something is giving way,
will not hold under this changed gravity —
        she feels her frame fretted raw
by the humming steel now keen to some subliminal chord
shaping itself within the quick of her skull.
        Almost, almost, scream or song finds tongue —

almost the knit bone is again undone,
  but sudden dawn filters the motes of her raised dust,
and the magnet spends its force. Dawn: the unheld dead
   drift again in our pilgrim eyes
  as we draw back, touch with restive hands
    our own braided skulls.

Cradling all that was not edible
The scooped-out shell lay steaming
In an empty field of sugar cane
Where we had dumped it after bringing

Turtles from the sea, dividing them
Among ourselves and dressing each
Ancient hulk in stealth for fear the law
Had seen and tracked us from the beach.

Cast-off vital parts grew black, then green,
And simmered in the Florida heat.
Buzzards circled, swooped, and took what parts
The dogs or wildcats would not eat.

Fang and beak devoured my flesh each night
Until the Cuban workers came,
Turned the spoil of rent and rotted heart
Onto the newly planted sugar cane.

The Final Reasoning of Kings

Cannon from another war
Are mounted on the parapet beyond my office door.
I can call them by their names,
Tell to strangers something of their range,
Their casting dates, explain the Latin of their kings —
ULTIMA RATIO REGUM it reads on each of them.
I point out further that as warriors
Once clept their swords,
So these wry Frenchmen dubbed their guns:
On one side play *La Lézarde, Le Carillon.*
On the other *Le Sévère, Le Tintamare,*
Grown old, withhold their bronze uproar.

In the middle of this all
Are larger, more fatal arms — *L'Envoi, L'Aurore.*
To come closer to this silent pair
Is to see two green serpents crawl
Along the top of each toward the sighting beads;
Their arching backs provide the slots
To carriage these progenitors.
One green serpent of the four
Has lost its head.
Was it clapped off in need of shot
Or greed of that war's token, this curious detail?

In either case, it lies forgetful
Of some soldier's open hand or broken skull,
Forgetful even of the serpent's tail,
For no sooner was the envoy's message gone
Than the other bore its savage light to dawn.

Water I Thought Sweet and Deep

The quail are flying wild
And those we've killed begin to smell
So we turn toward home
On a day too hot to hunt.

At some stranger's dog-trot shack
We ask if there is water we might drink.
A raw-eyed drunken man offers from a Mason jar
The same white whiskey that rings his rotten jaw.

We decline and find his well —
I draw and drink until
I see swimming in the dipper
Flukes in water I thought sweet and deep

Flukes swimming grey against the tin
Before I throw them straight into the sun
Take his jar   drink what smells of kerosene and month-old egg
Breathe deep and sweet in my hunting bag

And retch until each organ wrings
Itself of water
Quail death
Whiskey I thought sweet and deep.

No Fluid-Fed Governor

With my father I drive this low road
                out into darkness
Where swamps press in
On what we have taken.
Beyond canals on either side
We hear the thrumming pulse of heavy diesels
Pumping water off the land.
In our nights they possess what comes within their pull —
We leave them unmanned —
Silent governors control the gravity flow
Of fuel from overhead tanks
And hold all needles below red line.

Miles back we left the highway,
Turned onto this road of crushed shell.
We follow its chalk whiteness,
Listening for the troubled engine.

Each pumping station we pass
Tells of its control
Over a share of this night's water.
Not until we are deep in the land,
          where the road begins
             to give itself to swamp,
Do we find a diesel stalled.

It has ripped itself from the foundation,
Gone wild on fumes from an empty fuel tank —
          fumes no fluid-fed governor could command —
Some one of us allowed the fuel to run low;
By night the tank was emptied
Of all but vapor,

And vapor fed the sucking gut
That pushed its needles
Beyond the hold of any governor.

Black earth is churned up
From the concrete pad to where
It lies like a broken animal,
        the needles of its red eyes
                fixed steady on the sea-shell road.

LET NOT YOUR HART BE TRUBLE

For George Garrett

The horn of your silver bus
Sounds in the rocks and trees,
Black Saul of Tarsus turned Paul,
And you come telling
Under what tree and with what light
You were struck blind
And now see.

On faith and a curve, both blind,
You double-clutch and pass my car,
Hoping against the evidence
Of things not seen,
Or, should it appear from around this curve,
You trust the roadside rocks and trees
Will open like the sea.
That failing, you take the rock and wood
For what it gives.

Your pass is good, and made, I guess,
With the same thick hand that lettered
The words on your rear exit door:
LET NOT YOUR HART BE TRUBLE
You exact too much, black Paul,
My lane, my life on your faith,
My troubled hart.
And yet I do not deny you unlettered
The gift of metaphor, or even parable;
The master himself spoke thus,
Lest the heart of the many be softened.

You talk like you clutch, old black soul,
For you know the troubled hart
Takes the hunt
Into a deeper wood.

II. Other Sides

Rank on rank of false right eyes
Stared into my loss
And I saw
He would not find my soft brown eye,
Not in a thousand leather trays;
Not for all the purple velvet
That could be cut to lay them on
Was there an option
Able to resplit my sight
Or make me a king.
Not even his costly Orientals
Could fake my lost right eye.

He tried, eye after eye;
They lay like bogus coins
In my forehead.

Level with his window was a minaret
On whose globe he said
To fix my fluid left eye
For a truer fit.
As he ground with sand and steel
To shape blown glass to my blind side,
I saw again the world no longer turned
Around the sun,
Was flat, lacked depth,
Went neither beyond
Nor came before
The one-dimensional plane
Of sky and globe and minaret.

Into that vacancy
He placed the cold brown eye
My father paid him money for.
It was like a slug in the musicbox;
I could not play my song.
When I reached for things
They still were not there.

In the mirror beside his window
I tried again to find a true brown eye;
The truest there
Was in my father's saddened face.
Through the dark prosthetic glass
Vision came of my sovereign option:
I broke from his hand,
The stranger's vitreous smile, that humorless room,
And went into the park below.
Bell notes floated from the minaret
Like concentric waves in the fountain pool
Where I threw the mold-blown piece
And began to sort the planes,
Play the songs,
Between sky and globe and minaret,
Trusting depth to the patch of black
Behind my lost brown eye.

The Majorette on the Self-Rising Flour Sign

We came each day to where
You had been laid
In tall grass behind the football field,
Twice again as large as any half-time majorette.
Where you once stood and smiled beside our practice field
Some more comely figure had reared herself
To suggest we try her snowy white self-rising flour.
But she stood beyond our ready grasp;
You waited in easy weeds,
Offering the self-same flour.
Although your soldier-girl suit was out of style
We rose to the red, white, and blue of your flower,
Imagined ourselves clasped
Between your flaking white thighs,
And peeled the red away to see
What secrets lay beneath your uniform —
We found the galvanized lie,
Slowly peeled you all away,
And went to other flower fields.

From where we sit tonight
We do not see your skeleton in the weeds.
New floodlights now blaze above us
And players from another generation
Prepare their kick-off on this worried ground.
Dutifully we rise for The Star-Spangled Banner
And over the loudspeaker a prayer comes
For good clean sports.
Behind the top-row bleachers on less familiar signs
Are this age's superwomen,
Their painted smiles saying merely someone has the ball.

And now as half-time majorettes cover the grid
We go to the sideline cables for a closer look.
A new routine is announced.
But when the floodlights go off
Nothing new comes; our bloodshot eyes
Reject the dark, begin to probe beyond the field,
Catch on something, snatch and seize a form that parts the grass —
In our flaming hands on these retaining wires
We feel an old charge now current our night,
For you arise from those self-same weeds
And under goal posts take flesh
And come to where we hang on cables,
Breathless.

You pitch and toss across the field
And at the end throw your fire batons
Into the night —
We watch with galvanized eyes
As you come again full-fleshed
In these half-times of our lives.

Too near   too near
In memory are the fires
Across the lake
On Cypress Point:
We have our free ribs and beer
They theirs
Across the lake
In the flickering
Other half of our company
Barbecue.
At the water's edge
I watch and hear
First song
Blues   soul   tonk
Then shouts
And know
There is blood
This 4th of July night
Even among their own.
Monday there will be a blue
And cut-up Negro
On the line.
We work in steam and styrofoam
Side by side
At PolarTherm
Make Santa Claus masks
And reindeer in July
Surf boards and water jugs
In December
But no styrofoam
That I might mold
Could seal or float

Me far enough
To where I could
Not see their fires.
Through my Santa mask
I see them
Even on the water.

The Barber with the California Tan

California never saw a winter,
According to this barber at my back
Whose flagging leather long since ceased to temper
Any steel. His razor trembles at my neck.
Outside his window is a bogus barber pole;
The static stripes have never unrolled
And given themselves to a spiral
That would wind the eye into a flux more purgatorial.

He claims an eternal California tan,
Says he went there once to harvest citrus fruit.
For proof he rolls the sleeve of his nylon barber suit
And bares the hairless white arm of an aging man.
My strength about me on the floor, I rise
And leave him shuffling in the ashes of his burnt-out California eyes.

The Feather

The fish are leaping from the sea
And swallowing whole the gull, the kill dee,
                           and the fisher king.
On the waters float feathers one and four;
Dead fish fester on the shore.

Down the beach comes a child;
Her mouth is glad, her hair
                    blows wild.
She clutches fish in each hand
And toes at others on the sand.

She only takes the hard and dry;
The fetid ones she quickly culls,
For hot is the day
               and close the sky.
Low over the water fly the gulls.

The good, she says, will last for days
Under a tub in the shade
                  by her door.
On the waters float feathers one and four;
Dead fish fester on the shore.

To my why she says she does not know,
                        does not know,
Voice and vision distant, drifting
To the children down the beach,
Their morning laughter out of reach.

Of the feathers one and four
One is swept onto the shore.

She casts aside the fish
　　　　in one hand
And runs to the feather on the sand.

She grasps the up-turned feather
　　　　　　in one fist,
Four silvery fish in the other.
She does not see or hear the tide
Lapping up the footprints in her stride.

A noonday moon is sucking festered fish
　　　　　　　again into the sea
Where feathers float now only one and three.
She sees the waves are straining for the shore
But ebb away each time a little more.

　　　　On that increasing shore
She stoops and sticks the feather in the sand
And goes away with fish in hand
To the tub in the shade by her door.
It soon will wash away; it will not stand.

The Lame, the Halt, the Half-Blind

Each Sunday from my window
I see a one-legged, crippled man
Wheel his chair to a pay-phone booth below.
With my one good eye
I watch him grasp the ledge,
Lift himself into the booth, then pull inside
His lifeless leg.

I cannot hear the dial tone
Nor the ringing in a near
Or far-off room
Nor the words between this man and another,
But if my phone should ever ring
When he has dialed his number
I will lock my house against the nimble-limbed and total blind;

I will meet him in the street
Where gathered will be
The lame, the halt,
The half-blind. We shall dance, the one-eyed with the lame,
Singing; the deaf will hear our song
And come; in the country of the blind
We shall be making half-blind love,
King and court and countryside.

One Last Cheer for Punk Kincaid

We never believed that any judge's word
Could send Punk Kincaid to Parchman Farm,
But when Punk broke and wept
On the last night of his trial a year ago
We knew that he was guilty as accused
And never again would we run interference
As he brought back a down-field punt
Or took a hand-off on a sweeper play
And moved on out into an open field.
Today we are watching Negro trusties
Drag a lake near Parchman Farm
For his body.
Word had come that Punk went down
To help recover a drowned man;
We drove all morning into the Delta
Thinking he might rise grinning
Near the sidelines
And josh about this trick
He had pulled
Or simply say the names of towns
He cruised the rustled cattle through —
Anguilla, Rolling Fork, Redwood, on to Natchez —
And with the Negroes from the boat
Gathered with us in a circle
We would help him mile by mile
Through the outlaw past.
They drag the lake with net and hook
But it will not give him up —
Below their boat
The drowned are running interference
For Punk Kincaid
As he returns a punt
From deep inside his own territory.

Departure from the Waldorf

What states wait between here and home
become vague in the high alcoholic dark
where snow forms to fall on Park Avenue

And where what the open window holds
in the facing wing becomes the woman one loves
or could in dream love but for obscuring snow,

Appointed times, the palpable fall of one's body
through the rent floors of the Waldorf,
and finally this simultaneous arrival in the lobby —

From out of the snow float Thai,
Malays, or maybe Balinese in formal dress,
mingling dream, witness, event in ambience

Of color, motion, music. Caught in the high slant
of their lip song I go with them to dance
the slow, imagined dance of the Orient.

Valley of Dry Bones

Because of declining mineral resources, the United States may
eventually have to reprocess the metal in the 6 million auto-
mobiles it junks every year, a Federal official predicts.
—*The New York Times*

The bones of old Fords, Packards, Chevrolets,
Hudsons, Cadillacs, and Henry J's
Lie ash-dry in the valley.

There is a noise, behold, a rattling;
And the bones come together,
Tube to its tire, cap to its hub,
Universal to its joint.

And as I look there is chrome
Come upon them, lacquer, coat upon coat,
And they breathe, these slain,
That they may move.
Son of man, can these bones live?

III. Light-Hearted

In My Secret Iago Heart
or
Renal Calculus

Cloaked in what time's variorum has given me
I keep silence, yet note well
From my place behind this room's arras
What is said of my, Iago's, motivation.

I hear how exigencies created my guile,
A mere stage villain, or how I, some anti-logos
Become flesh, played yet another Satan
Among the innocent.

A bearded man argues for my incipient homosexuality,
Reaches for the water glass
And passes on the microphone to a tempestuous
Lady critic who is keen on my artistic bent.

Finally the argument narrows to the Renaissance Man
Who sees me as a Machiavel
And the man who says I merely had
An unusually sharp renal calculus.

Before Questions & Answers I steal out,
Honest, honest in my secret Iago heart.

The Adoration of the Magi

In the midst of all this sacred
Adulation, what is the meaning of these naked
Youths, florid birds, and uncouth beasts?
The star that brought them to the East,
Where does it shine, Angelico?
If flesh's music plays this rondo,
Where sings the soul?
"Why call one part the whole,"
A lusty voice replies,
"It is I, Lippo Lippi, who defy
The circumscription of such holiness
As Word made flesh."
He shouts this from some whorehouse door
And says for me to take my further doubts before
The gewgaw oracle that he has placed on Jesus' thigh
Where it grins at kneeling magi.

My Dog and I Grow Fat

For Curtisy, Barnaby, & Plum

His true grace, the dog books hold,
Is witnessed only in the field,
And I suppose our yard's
A field of sorts —
His Irish eye is smiling on the sparrow there,
He stalks the squirrel as a king's dog would exotic birds,
And springs like bright wire
After butterflies,
Wildly outside his droll household self.
He takes their minor flights as threats against
His bones, yet is able only to wolf
An occasional loose feather or taste of butterfly dust.

My crew-cut neighbor hints
It's a shame he's not been trained to hunt,
Says it'd lean him down
And he wouldn't grow dull.
He's gun shy, I say, can't hold a point.
Our talk dwindles to the time he's having with his crew-cut lawn,
The drought.
We ease away, I to these poems,
My dog to our riot of weeds.
When the neighbor is inside
I write a poem wherein my dog
And I grow fat on butterfly dust.

Tonight we chase the lightning bugs
To work off fat and keep from growing dull.

No Doric Air

I am prepared now and will be during the winter period to take care of pupils in either Latin, Greek, English, History, or Mathematics. The Mathematics would embrace all grades from the 5th and 6th up through the algebras, Plane Geometry, and Trigonometry.
—*A recent notice among the want ads of a Southern small-town newspaper.*

By which Ionic foot, greater or lesser,
kind doctor, will you tame the Southern *agricolae*
you see tomorrow bringing to your magnolia grove?

No Doric air stirs this Sunday afternoon,
these green waxen leaves shading fluted stone,
or the portico where, liveried in grey senility,
you wait to usher in the *tabulae rasae.*

From our air-conditioned Detroit car
we wave; you nod, thinking pupils have come early
to read of Xenophon's anabasis, Caesar's legions,
learn how *Gallia est omnis divisa in partes tres,*
and play that old Pythagorean rag.

I Circle the Midway

With my transistor radio by my side
I go from ride to ride —
The Ferris Wheel, the Silver Bullet, the Tiltawhirl.
I fly like a wild mad one-eyed dove
    to the arms of the roller-coaster girl,
Go with lovers laughing through the Tunnel of Love,
And wait with little girls wailing
        for another spin
On the Merry-Go-Round.
I know the way of carnival things
    which always end
    where they begin,
Know the earth's recall
    equals each ascent, know the rising fall.

Yet every year on this day
I circle the midway
In my motorless one-winged plane at the Mid-South Fair,
And with a magic wind in my hair
I lean out over the cockpit rail,
Hail the sideshow blondes in blue fiberglass veils
      and pink high heels,
Pass low and set a glister in each tart's eye,
Lay down sparks in every virgin's heart, I
    touch the old with lust
And to every woman's daughter say
This is not the last of my solo flights;
If you weren't old enough to ride the ride
    of your desire,

Come again next year
As I circle the midway
  with my transistor radio by my side.

Zannie Hayes dug in the dark, hard earth
For a dollar and a dime an hour,
Time and a half for overtime,
Until one Sunday when her people were away
His woman asked him if he'd like
        To come in for sweetbread and wine.

Zannie Hayes, though strong from digging in the dark, hard earth,
Trembled all the way across her yard,
Stumbled up the front door steps,
And was on the porch before he finally said
He believed he would
        Come in for sweetbread and wine.

Zannie Hayes who dug in the dark, hard earth
For a dollar and a dime an hour,
Time and a half for overtime,
Now plows his father-in-law's fields
For a dollar and a dime a day,
        Sweetbread and wine for overtime.

Lines Composed a Few Miles below Princeton Junction

Sleepless in my sleeping car,
Pulled horizontal over railings
Which are twisting, jerking, throwing light
                              fantastic sparks
To the shuffling earth,
I discover all dark's eyes as being
                    either red or white;
Nothing blue or green in this night
                   betrays the day.

At some small hour and place
                   beside the tracks
A mobile home on cinder blocks
                rolls and rocks
To beats and wailings withheld from me,
As I pass soundless in compartmental dark
                 those sleepless faces
                 and blazing windows
Where others less inclined than I
Are dancing, dancing,
                dancing out the night.

iv. Turnings

Were You Wise, Awake?

Reading me like an old tale of desire,
My one eye, its twisting dream,
Was full knowledge your possession?
Reading by fire, were you wise, awake?
What knowing was there
Your hand, in sleep, on the flame
Could not more willfully bring?
Your conch beside the fire
Sings its desire, yet sings no such fury
As the quickened one
In the moon's half-light or in the torn eye of the sun
Beneath the turning sea.
Let us come together some darkness — night or noon —
Compare in fire and water our wounds.

The Starlings

The starlings leave the trees and come to peck
At crumbs, hard and stale as cinder rocks,
On the snow beneath the Kotex box
Which a stick is propping up.

A string jerks taut,
The stick flicks out,
Children run and hover near the fallen box,
Hearing that beating from within, soft and frantic.

Hands grope up under the edges;
Each gets a bird, some two,
Because to hold a thing that flies is flight
Itself. They hold their birds in close and tight,

But soon they feel the wax run hot and soft
And know with Icarus the purchase lost.
They fling their starlings up. Their flight, their fall,
Is like the box, of which they only know

It has to do with women's secret places.

The Room

Again in dream
On stairs winding upward
Toward promises
Of light and long halls
Of high-ceilinged rooms
I move out of darkness.
I ascend and stand wax-kneed
Before a door,
Fumbling to fit key into case.
The clumsy tumblers fall in place
And the bolt is drawn,
Emitting a clack which gambols
The length of the hall,
Proclaiming this violation.
I wait to glimpse
Some thing come slobbering,
Raging forth, child-hungry,
But it does not show itself.

Inside the room is the cunning —
There are two doors,
One to a closet,
The other to another room.
Thinking to trap me
In the other room,
It does not rush
But lurks inside the closet.
I jerk the closet door half open,
Throw my body back against it,
Then open the door fully
To see the fallen creature
And am seized in the coils

Of my own constricting muscles —
It hovers there in darkness,
Long and black.

Dreams and wakings pass
Before I see this thing
For what it is —
A long black overcoat
Hanging on a coat hanger.
I take it down
And in a pocket find
A straight razor
With concaved blade
And handle of bone,
Cased neatly in a thin
Handcrafted wooden box.
It is honed against the dark
Behind my child's face,
Waking to the dream
Of another door,
Another room.

Else Birth Make Us Husband

I have dreamed birth again
    from the mother tree of thorns,
have seen flesh issue from the vulvaed bark
        above earth
where an older boy wiped his man-stuff
    wrung out for my schooling
beyond the apple core and cinder yard.

In his father's tree
he had matched his fish's one eye
    against the sun's,
ghosting my single ignorant eye
into that ritual of proof
   bound by the cloth of his sun hut
high above our neighbors' circumspection.

Birth I knew formed in all
    the sun shone on
and there in his hand spilled seed
    from the thwarted blood of his lust,
going into the wood where already birth's foreshadowing
      unsettled my brain's clay.

To earth, slat by slat,
    to my landlocked, oblate street of sheetrock houses,
and then dream of birth:
Birth, in the wood, of the thorn-suffered creature,
breaking from bark like fire
    over that asbestos circle,
come supplicant into my unfatherly dreams
which allowed only love's coming
      to scald my loins,

no neighbor's creation of thorny flesh
claiming my palm's warmth, the cradle of my wonder,
for there was birth in my own hand
of the man-fluid,
and proof of the hair-making water
under my arm, growing singly,
a promise of love strength
to any neighbor's daughter,
there to be seen in waking —
Only half-formed, the knowledge,
that we lay deep our seed in love's dream
or throw it free
else birth make us husband
to the thorny tree.

The Pomegranate

It was to be no day of common fruit,
We knew, when Champ descended from his yellow bus
To schoolyard cinders,
Coming from out in the country,
        somewhere near the river,
Where each season yielded
      some new token
By which he held us to his slanted course.

No paper page was more read that morning
Than that of the large brown bag
In Champ's cubbyhole
        and none more blank.
But in our deepest body
We were waking to the votive stir
          of seed within seed.

Recess came and we entered
That random yard of cinders
Which today heard only our hushed voices
          and our beating blood.
We stood ready with common fruit
     to offer for a taste of pomegranate flesh.

With familiar hands
He plucked the crown of calyx lobes
And sank his fingers into the rind,
      opening to us the berried chambers
A summer heat had seeded.
Our hands went out, our blood caught and rose,

The strung wires of our nerve sang
                                a new wind,
And our teeth were set on edge
                                by small grenades of sweetness.

Seeing that more had come than could *have,*
Champ threw the remaining fruit into our midst
And took away
                our red and golden apples,
Leaving us with a lingering sweet acid taste
                                and cinders in our knees.

II

Before our chemistries surged us
                beyond his dazzling ciphers,
Before error forced us to trial,
We were locked further in the images of his lore:
After the pomegranate,
He muscled us with the dry ball of fur and bone
He brought to biology, a small hare
Regurgitated by the owl,
                and yet we are wiser
For having held the artifacts
That took shape in our hands
As he conjured out of mere traces
                a grotesque vision of the whole — the bleached snake
Bottled in alcohol,
                the egg it ate intact;
The viper eyes, the bulge, something our book
Could not rightfully illustrate.
Nor could it properly tell
The fragile mystery of the flying squirrel
                smothered in his unvented lard pail
Or of the hornet's nest we gave our lunch money for.

Drawn week by week
         into his rural sophistry,
Unable to break the stark analogies,
We were browbeat
Until we began to see into a world
             where the true word
Rarely found its rightful image.
That discovered, we began to cipher
The meaning of the expanding rebus
He drew.

Slowly most of us have come free
Of his twisted tales — of how hogs copulate
Or word of the literal "calm" that would flow
         from between the legs of manic backwood girls
     to warm him
Or any at the flush moment.
And yet how many sought in their souped-up coupes
         for that issue or some other impossibility of flesh
Long after he lost
     his grade school hold?

Or seek still? — for it was no simple overthrow.
It is the images that most forcefully outlive
     their past,
Impending as he appears again,
             the ghost of a face home on leave,
Stoned on vodka,
         lost somewhere in the twistings of his own myth.
In the snarl of memory
             a single vision
Defies his damages:
         one oblique morning
     when promise came of the seed's fruition.

There has been no death
      as fruitful as his
In that small war.

Ring, Chain, Coin

For Lucy

Despite the keys
The image is no less visible
Than on the night you gave it
(The profiled regard no less certain,
This IMPerator MAXIMINUS PIUS AUGustus
Whose hidden obverse eye
Looks through the coin
To his own legend, then beyond
To ours.)
I repeat his stare into the coin,
Then beyond, meeting the limits of his vision
But making time
Come round,
Remembering *you, the night, its gift* —

The keys, you knew, would be attached
To the ring and thus to the coin
By the slender silver chain
And there would be the rub:
In my pockets the keys would work against the image
Until with time there would be but a blur
Where once were well defined lines.

Reluctant to break
The coin from the chain,
I let that erasure of time,
Like dream, go on,
Turning a blind eye also to the legend
I saw forming on the soft coin of our nights.
I'd had three seasons within your door —

Fall, winter, spring —
Yet now was unwilling to accept
My own face in the design those seasons shaped.
I promised myself that soon
A conclusion would be found
And your key returned —
Further, I would be shed of all keys.

By June the keys were hanging
Silent beside their latches,
I was in another city,
And the ring seemed free.

But the ring, of course, is never free.
The doors we enter
Will open
Only as they opened for this Thracian
Who for three years held the keys to empire
And had coins struck with his one-eyed gaze:
They open with keys
And into ironies
Too simple and fitting for belief.
Another place frees us
Of nothing but the presence of faces
That have dreamed us in the coin
We could not fit —
Or still another place, of the presence of those
That we have dreamed
And lost in our own.

And so I have detached the coin,
Put it on a chain of finer links,
Carry it elsewhere about me
Rather than think of rooms
Where silver dust was all I left.

We leave only money
Or love;
I leave you this:
On both sides of the coin
I have seen how complicities of time
And desire
Impel us through histories others suffer in —
And have been helpless
As if locked in love.

The Bells

In an exit of nets
        that form a cone into the night
The overhanging bells
                offer themselves
To the many small hands.
      A mash of noise
             builds in the funnel's lip
      and swells into the netted flare
      as we mill through the gates,
Our festival of the arts now finished,
Except for the many
           small hands
        sweeping across the bells,
        grating broken-glass-like
           on my ears.
I am nearly past the gates
           and free
When out of the crowd
      she steps,
      a child on tiptoe,
           and with extended
                  finger
touches a single
        bell,
      releasing on the chill air
        a sound quavering still toward where facing mirrors
                          meet.
And I
      with others
           under over-
              hanging bells

      want to touch
          Her
             so sweeping
But am held
In crowding nights of bodies mashed
                 also with many small hands.

The Gars

The fire and Sam Boy's voice
Kept us warm, dry, safe
From the night.

No breath was allowed to shadows
There, for shadows die, never are,
No objects given,

And we had built on sand,
No standing thing near, our fire
Of driftwood, dried
From sun of day
Since the river left her bed
In an older, wilder time,
                                   Away from here
                                   Away from here.

Sam Boy drank white whiskey
From a Clorox jug and told
Of other times,
                        Away from here.

Little Brother listened,

And Culler walked in the night, looking.

The dogs struck and told us so.
Sam Boy said put out the fire,
Follow the dogs,
                        Get away from here.

The dogs told us strong again
The woods were wet and the coon scent

Was holding good,
                    Come away from there.

But Culler walked in the night, looking.

Little Brother said the nights
Got darker as the month wore on
And the month was old.

The fire was out, the dark moved in.
Sam Boy had the carbide lit
And Culler said
                    Over here.

It was the river's old bed
We had to ford, but Culler found
A log across.

The carbide light slashed the dark
And was true,
Truer than a lying fire,
For it was moving
                    Away from here.

But Culler stood in the night, looking,
Looking down into waters darker
Than old, old months.

Sam Boy shined the log,
Said it's a slick walk
And the water's deep.

The light spilled over the log,
Caught a moving shadow, then another,
And another.

The gars darted to the light, flitting
Long and thin, rodlike seeds
Of an older night,
                    Away from here
                    Away from here.

Night-dammed waters from unknown times
Suddenly broke and churned
In Culler's skull.

And Culler crouched quick in the night, looking,
Said shine the light, Sam Boy,
                    Over here.

Culler thrust the shotgun
Into the water and let go
Both barrels.

Waters may part for wooden staff,
But not for ancient gun of twisted
Damascus steel.

The whole night blew up,
Flew out of socket
And spun,
Knocked Little Brother off the log,
Threw Sam Boy back
On the sand.

Little Brother was in the water
Hollering like a bad dream
Had him,
And Sam Boy,
    eyes wild
    unhearing ears,
Groped for a pole.

Away in the woods
The dogs heard and bayed back
   for a word,
     a sign,
      a sound.
And got only an echo,
    a shadow,
   No word, no word.

And Culler runs in the night, looking,
     Away from here
     Away from here.

AIR HERO KILLED IN FREAK CRASH
—*The Panolian,* Panola County,
Mississippi, April 22, 1943

Over Pacific waters far from your mother's
cotton farm in Panola County
you rode Jap flak by sun or star,
went 68 times above the small enemy.

In February the target had been Rabaul
where you took your Fortress in
for nearly five hours, flying never above
4700 to keep the eye of the yellow dog at a slant.

A month before with a single bomb
you sank two ships of the Rising Sun,
planting your half-ton missile
between a destroyer tender and a smaller vessel
moored alongside, blasting both ships
completely out of the water.
Also "a master craftsman at the art of skip-
bombing," according to your commander.

That Pacific winter behind, you went into spring
a hero, leading your own squadron,
credited with the sinking
of more than 20 Japanese warships or merchantmen.

And then one night in April
a little wallaby sped across the airdrome
directly in the path of your death-heavy B-17
and got caught in a wheel.

All that to have some small creature,
which came not fully nourished from its mother's water
and crawled to pull at life inside her pouch
until strong enough to run through
darkness toward other waters,
come softly against your rubber,
break hydraulic lines and send fluid spewing
into the flared exhaust. You sat unbelieving,

strapped in the pilot's seat
while fire picked clean your cotton-soft
hair and your own bombs blasted
completely out of you the water of life.

The Day Speedo Stole the Meat Wagon

Out of some wrong sleep
Snatched in unlocked car, under truck
Or viaduct, or in strange doorway
Speedo crawled and came to keep,
When the thought or need struck,
His vague engagement with chill trays
Of ladled brain, slabs of meat,
And stacks of liver, tongue, and pigs feet.

Leaving his trail of slobber, hog snot, and gall
From butcher block to meat wagon,
He shambled over saw dust floors
And raged that we would one and all
Rot in hell, be ate by dragons —
Our eyes, organs, everything right down to heart's core —
And come out their dragon butts in little balls of burning muck
For working him so and not letting him drive the delivery truck.

We burned in Speedo's dreams;
He blackened our working days,
Fouling all he named or touched,
Smiling only when he schemed.
He began to grin for days, spilled half his trays,
Then disappeared; our driver found him crouched
Inside a full delivery truck, gnawing on a bone.
It was the day Speedo stole the meat wagon.

No longer do dark corners of our packing plant
Reek of what he stopped there for.
But still somewhere each night an open car
Or strange doorway shadows him in this or another town.
The only word we have is from a fisherman

Whose nets were near where Speedo left the truck.
He said that judging from the gore and ruck
It looked to have been a feast of the giants.

"Does Anybody Wanna Buy My Little Brother?"

With my camera
I am waiting
For the roof
Where today, with luck,
I will shoot
The single white pigeon.
At street level
The red-tile roof lines
Run like cotton rows
Seen from a passing car,
Parallel lines that move
Toward where the pigeon's wing
Touches finally down,
Flight ends.
I will shoot the bird
At rest where converging lines
Begin to suggest, come near,
Final things.

Beside me a little man
Talks incessantly on,
Having broken the covenant
That exists unspoken
Between commuters
On this city bus.
I am waiting,
Wishing silence,
But he nudges and points:
"Over there once were empty lots."
Bread trucks now wait row upon row.
"And there, right there," he tells me,
"Was a white house

With a fierce chow dog out front
That waited for me to pass each day."
I see a laundromat
Where the city's linen
Is spinning dry —
"And down there is the corner,
The corner!" he says,
"Where my brother held me
By the hand and hollered
'Does anybody wanna buy my little brother?' "
The white pigeon,
The white pigeon
Is fixed in silence
On the roof.
I set the f/stop,
Focus,
Am about to trip
The shutter,
Admit light,
Stop time,
The pigeon's wing —
He jerks me around,
The camera swings —
He is weeping,
Saying over and over
His brother's words,
"Does anybody wanna buy my little brother?"

In my darkroom
The print registers
Clear sky,
A telephone line
Diagonally across one corner,
And faintly
The wing of a bird.

The Dove

Beyond his need of flesh
She rested in the field's lone tree, yet he would flush
Her into the simple wind that rustled husks
And raised a small grey dust

As he stalked along the row,
Seeking closer range,
For even at a stone's throw
It was not a killing gun, his .28-gauge —

More a bastard gun, loaded only for skeet
And spreading shot like sleet
From a sawed-off, chokeless barrel
Wild with patterns that cripple more than kill.

All sounds were kept among the gathered stalks
Except the clicking hammer-cock,
The roar, and pellets clawing air like angry hawks.

She was spread-wing in mid-air
When the load caught full flare
And feathers flew like puffweed seeds as she, that hung
Once weightless, fell now leaded as an unstrung plumb.

Power came with ease and glory fast across that sweeping
Space where he moved toward dying, lost in dust,
Lost, then cut to the quick, made alive, as she opened her wings,
Caught air, shook it off and caught

Again, not even head-high off
The ground. She got a hold on air, on life,
And pulled, pulled strong across
The creek, into the waiting trees.

Languages We Are Not Born To

Can we hear with a different ear the sounds
That bolted from your inarticulate jaw,
Can we call back our laughter
That burned your eyes to salt,
Now that you speak in another tongue
And make of speech a song?

You came with fractious talk
        from a broken mobile home,
And tried with maladroit tongue to answer questions
Posed in the language that those around you spoke,
Tried until you learned that languages we are born to
        are not always our own.

Having stumbled into a foreign tongue
And stilled the stutter
That broke your native speech,
Can you give us now some word
To quiet the flutter
Which works unheard
On our own hidden lips and tongues?

The Big Money Comes to My Hometown

They have done
well where I once
worked for minimum wage
on the graveyard
shift and learned the hours
of the Mississippi dark.
We made what served a leisure
people in their off-time hours —
ice buckets, camp stoves,
portable reclining chairs.
But the dies,
I read today,
are being cast
for different tempered steel.
The hometown paper says
POLARTHERM GETS
MULTI-MILLION DOLLAR
CONTRACT. And in lower-case letters:
To Make Bomb Fins
For US Defense
Dep't.   Just as soon
as machines are retooled
from 100 to
200 additional persons will work my shift
for minimum wage
and learn to watch
the small, grave hours
of the dark.

The Bluebottle Tree

Through years of fear and midnight wrath you've wrestled
Bat-winged things, fled
The fast white spiders and tried to outshout
The loud gods; mornings
                    come uneasy.
The bottle pile beside your shotgun house
Grows bigger — empty bottles: the beers are brown,
The whiskeys clear, and milk of magnesia
                    comes in bottles of translucent blue.
But on this summer day you've cut a green bay tree,
Sheared the leaves away, stubbed the branches,
Stuck it upright in your yard, yard that it is,
And slipped bottles over the stubs,
                    many blue bottles.

Blueblazing in three o'clock sun
Above the raw rusted gulley,
It blares in elemental glory,
Your bluebottle tree, a hard-won
Stay against confusion,
Bought with gnawed-out bellies
Like those of Giacometti's
Models, mere cinders of the sun.
Must these always be the terms?
Do ulcers, worms, or utter fear
Have to be the roots of your blue word?
And yet you grin, and in grinning affirm,
Through haze of magnesia, whiskey, or beer,
That you have a tree fit for a golden bird.

Kelly Dug a Hole

I set the stakes,
Stretched the twine,
Told my labor crew
How deep, how wide to go,
Told them not to twist
Or bend their holes,
Not to bring them
To a point or flare
Because we'd have
To have the bottoms
Square and flat
To pour the footings
Where a building
Would finally stand.
Other workers flared,
Caved in the walls,
Or bent theirs
Out of shape,
But Kelly dug
And kept his straight,
Dug fifteen feet
Into a hill
The dozer missed.
When Kelly got on grade
I dropped the plumb
To check his hole.
At the top
I held the string
Three inches from the edge;
Down below
The plumb-bob
Ceased its swing

Three inches from the wall
And told me
Kelly's hole was true.
We built in ice and heat;
We built a building
Five stories high
In Oxford, Mississippi.
The walls and floors
Are spider-cracked in places
From some slight shifting,
But the building stands
And if any part will hold
When things begin
To slide and fall
That part will be
Where Kelly dug his hole.

Circling the Reef

Casting without charts for the fertile reef,
we prowl beyond sight
          of land or boat,
our Bendix depth-recorder
tuned to sound and graph
the vast erratic pulse of earth's relief.
The steady rise of the needle line
          on its unreeling cylinder
slows us to a troll, and making circles
               we pull our silver lures
                    through tropic streams
          where blood schools at the heart of its deepest dream.

The taloned hooks were mullet-baited
And dropped into the glacial
Brilliance where old night awaited
New day in waters crystal-
Green beneath our whiteflashing bow.
Spiraling up it came in troll
Toward our knifenosed prow,
Had taken the mullet whole
And came as a gift, however dumb
Or knowing,
From the seawomb.
But following
Its invisible helix came others
Of rainbow colors,
Free, yet caught in all the prisms of the sea.

Moonwing

Tonight with gin from a plastic glass
    and jet whispers of luck and love
in my ear, dreaming the deltas
  of these uniformed girls,
I round out another round trip
with no charm but the leaf
  I shape in the silver clover
    of this moonwing
outside the cone of my seatlight.
It is a dream of luck
    shaped against the fact
  that there is no promise
stronger than our unbroken contrails
      dissolving into what holds this thin purchase.

A need *to be somewhere*
     always above it
mothers invention,
  then hurls us through all weathers in its metal.
Watching dials,
    holding shafts of alloy,
  we dream
they will be true to our strictest maps
and forecastings.

Within one invented shell, another:
From the air today
    through plexiglass
I saw life run out
    in holiday colors
  on luck's stone clover;
on our fondest configuration of luck

and love
two cars came together.
It was a death that had no time or place
    but in my mind,
a vision invented out of need, the mind
    in doubt
saving itself at even that malicious cost.
We must see that
or a likeness thereof
  to be somewhere always
    above it.
That and more: the voyeur within,
        without whose invention we plunge,
must hear some ample voice
    say there are lights
of a city below us, we are in friendly skies.
    A mask will drop
       before our face
    if needed;
we are shown, ah desire,
    how to breathe!
We have these things around us.

The ice of doubt dissolves
    to watered gin —
surely the troth of these woman-soft voices
    cannot be broken;
they shall arrive unharmed
      at their small cars in the city
and I at mine, I tell myself, trying to outdistance
    today's vision of death on the cloverleaf, configurations
      of time and place
seen through plexiglass.

But there is turbulence
and only what is near me blurs
as I return my seat to its upright position,
    hoping we are hitting on all four
  in the dark over Memphis,
wondering what figure of love
    carries in laminated plastic
      or between pages
    the four-leaf and
      single stem
of my afternoon's clover.

DIAL DIRECT

At the Tri-State Fair and Exposition one year
I walked into a booth of color telephones
And lights which flashing spelled
                        DIAL DIRECT.

A smiling man with a microphone
Came down into the crowd
And, failing to reach those fearing
Some enormous joke, chose me
                        to dial direct
At company expense any man,
Woman, or child my heart desired.

To be so singled out
Brought to my head the rush and suck
Of wind on midway rides
And to my vision
                        a man whose face
Existed purely in the tilt and whirl
                        of a child's carnival world.

I said his name
Whom I had not seen or spoken to
Since I left his providing for,
                        whether in plenty or want,
Said in anger that the cost
Of his moving from state to state
Outweighed any found increase,
Shamed him for neglect, and left,
Only to learn the weight of stillness
                        and how in motion the soul grows light.

I took the telephone
and dialed my father direct.

Turning toward Song

With your dimestore compass
You lead us into woods
You say have not been hunted
Since slave times when your father
Brought his white men here
To hunt a meaner game.

Out in the night our dogs
Work trails deep into the woods
As we wait beside the fire,
Listening for them to tree.

When their frenzied song
Sounds from far away
We drown the fire,
And follow you over unmapped ground,
Giving ourselves unspoken to your direction
As you stop, scan the dial,
And turn toward song,

Reading all that comes within the compass
Of this groundless night
Whose quadrants shift
With each movement we make
Toward the heart
Of still another wood
You say no man has hunted.

Distinguished contemporary poetry in hardbound and paperback editions

ALAN ANSEN: *Disorderly Houses* (1961)

JOHN ASHBERY: *The Tennis Court Oath* (1962)

ROBERT BAGG: *Madonna of the Cello* (1961)

MICHAEL BENEDIKT: *The Body* (1968)

ROBERT BLY: *Silence in the Snowy Fields* (1962)

GRAY BURR: *A Choice of Attitudes* (1969)

TURNER CASSITY: *Watchboy, What of the Night?* (1966)

TRAM COMBS: *saint thomas. poems.* (1965)

DONALD DAVIE: *New and Selected Poems* (1961); *Events and Wisdoms* (1965)

JAMES DICKEY: *Drowning With Others* (1962); *Helmets* (1964); *Buckdancer's Choice* (1965) [National Book Award in Poetry, 1966]

DAVID FERRY: *On the Way to the Island* (1960)

ROBERT FRANCIS: *The Orb Weaver* (1960)

JOHN HAINES: *Winter News* (1966)

EDWIN HONIG: *Spring Journal: Poems* (1968)

RICHARD HOWARD: *Quantities* (1962); *The Damages* (1967)

BARBARA HOWES: *Light and Dark* (1959)

DAVID IGNATOW: *Say Pardon* (1961); *Figures of the Human* (1964); *Rescue the Dead* (1968)

DONALD JUSTICE: *The Summer Anniversaries* (1960) [A Lamont Poetry Selection]; *Night Light* (1967)

CHESTER KALLMAN: *Absent and Present* (1963)

CHARLES LEVENDOSKY: *perimeters* (1970)

PHILIP LEVINE: *Not This Pig* (1968)

LOU LIPSITZ: *Cold Water* (1967)

JOSEPHINE MILES: *Kinds of Affection* (1967)

Vassar Miller: *Wage War on Silence* (1960); *My Bones Being Wiser* (1963); *Onions and Roses* (1968)

W. R. Moses: *Identities* (1965)

Leonard Nathan: *The Day the Perfect Speakers Left* (1969)

Donald Petersen: *The Spectral Boy* (1964)

Marge Piercy: *Breaking Camp* (1968); *Hard Loving* (1969)

Hyam Plutzik: *Apples from Shinar* (1959)

Vern Rutsala: *The Window* (1964)

James Seay: *Let Not Your Hart* (1970)

Harvey Shapiro: *Battle Report* (1966)

Jon Silkin: *Poems New and Selected* (1966)

Louis Simpson: *A Dream of Governors* (1959); *At the End of the Open Road* (1963) [Pulitzer Prize in Poetry, 1964]

Anne Stevenson: *Reversals* (1969)

Richard Tillinghast: *Sleep Watch* (1969)

Charles Wright: *The Grave of the Right Hand* (1970)

James Wright: *Saint Judas* (1959); *The Branch Will Not Break* (1963); *Shall We Gather at the River* (1968)